Why **hellooo** there!

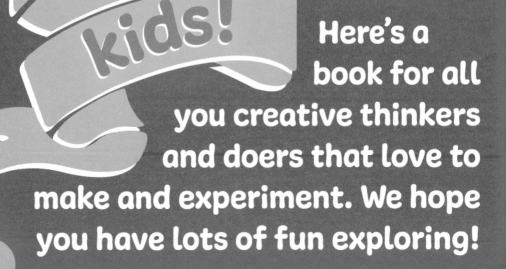

Welcome creative kids!

Here's a book for all you creative thinkers and doers that love to make and experiment. We hope you have lots of fun exploring!

1. Make a collage out of scraps from other crafts. You could even have a root through your recycling bin, your old sewing box, and find some exciting materials

Then jumble them to-gether and scan them, or even lay them on the floor and take a photo from up high

How many patterns can you invent from the scraps? Do the shapes remind you of anything, maybe an animal or a face?

2.

Make a big blobby painting! Go as big as you like, maybe even as big as a small island

Do lots of varied abstract shapes!

Why not make your

Here's some help for how:

Get a ball of clay and press your thumb into the middle of it, creating a start point. Then, using your thumb and fingers, pinch the clay to spread it out and go around, making a bowl shape. From here you can manipulate the clay as you like! You can add smaller chunks of clay and smooth those on to help give your pot height Play with the shapes you make! When you're happy, roll two sausage shapes and smooth one on each side for your handles!

3.

very own trophy!

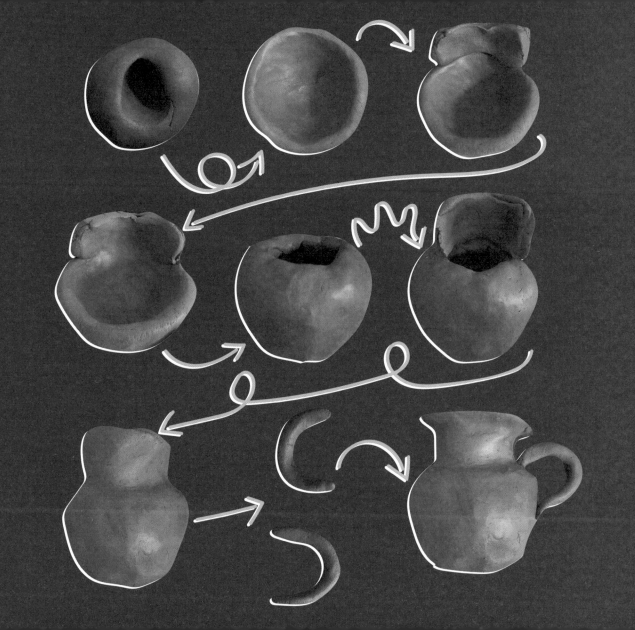

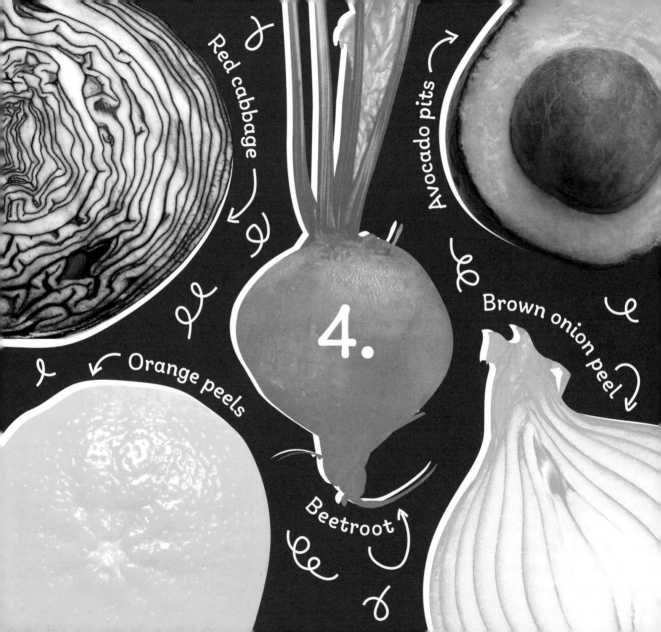

Red cabbage

Avocado pits

Brown onion peel

4.

Orange peels

Beetroot

Cut up your vegetables into small chunks + add them to a saucepan with cold water that only just covers them. Bring this to the boil then let it simmer for an hour.

To dye fabric, you need to prepare it for the dye. This is called a 'mordant'. You do this by dissolving the alum into boiling water. You need 2 teaspoons of alum for every 100g of fabric you want to mordant.

Once it's dissolved, add this to a large pot of hot water from the tap, and then add the fabric in. Let it soak for 45 minutes.

When you're ready to dye, rinse out all the mordant and put your fabric into the dye bath.

You've made your own dye

What colours did you get? If you leave the fabric in the dye for longer, does the colour get darker?

Why don't you try adding lemon juice to the cabbage dye!

Find some patterned or painted glasses in your home and place them in the sun- light.

Look at the <u>cool shadows!</u>

How many different shapes and patterns can you see? Can you draw them?___✏

Put some blobs of paint on some paper or even a canvas if you have one. You can use your favourite colours and can put the blobs where ever you like. Now take something flat and sturdy, like a ruler, and scrape it across the blobs! Keep a firm hold.

6.

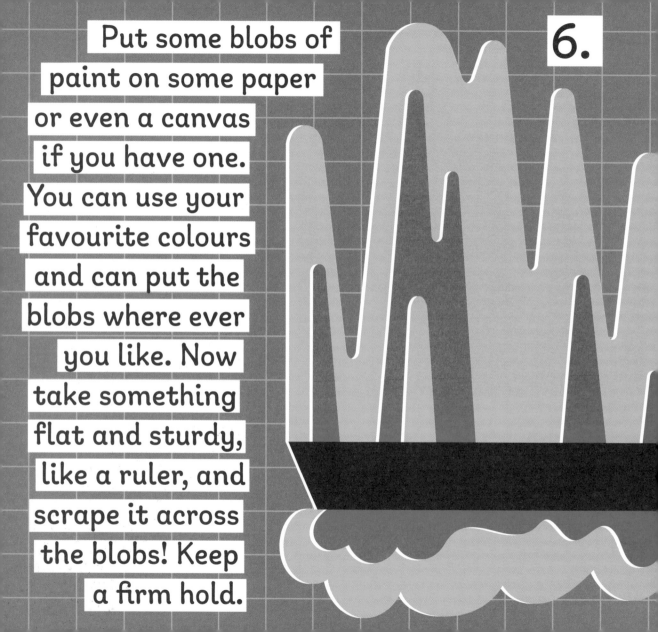

What does your painting look like?

Did you make any new colours?

7.

Experiment with puffy paint!

Here's how you make it:
1/4 cup of white glue
1/4 cup of shaving cream
Food colouring

Mix all of the ingredients starting with the glue first into a small container. Make a new little pot for each colour you want to make! Use a normal painting brush and paint to your heart's content!

8.

Test out how colours reflect by taking photos of the sun shining through stained glass, or even by making your own!

Mix water and paint or food colouring to make a super watery paint mix and freeze it.

What does the light look like shining through?
What happens if you hold a glass of juice up to the sunlight?

Imagine how colourful this would be with the sunshine!

What sculptures can you make? Cut out these shapes and slot them together in as many ways as you can.

9.

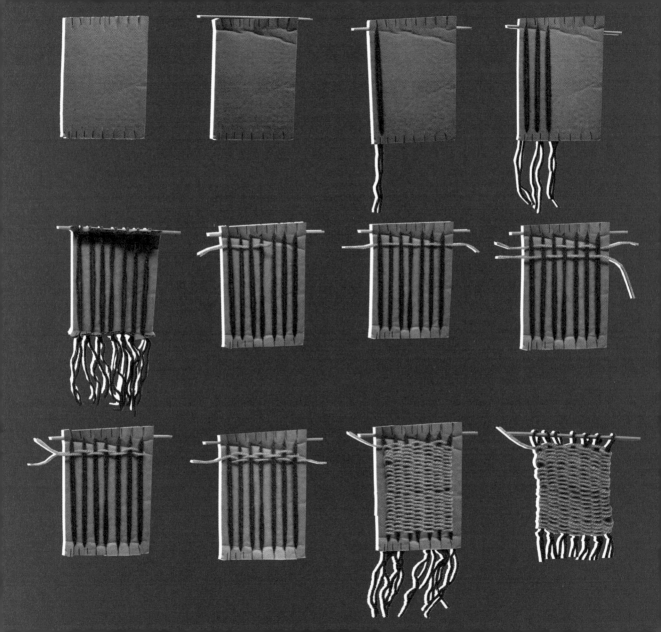

Make some decorative weaving!

Loop some strands of wool over a
stick or twig and let them hang down.
Fasten this onto a piece of cardboard
and cut some slits at the bottom to
pull the wool through to secure it.
This is called the 'warp'. Now you can weave!
Take a nice colour wool and start by
going under the first strand, then over
the second, under again, over, under, until
you get to the end of the strands! This is called
the 'weft'. For the next row of weft, take another
colour or the same one, if you like, and start by
going over, then under, and continue - you
should be doing the opposite to the last row.
And there you go! Continue this pattern to
the end of the woold strands and tie the
bottoms together, to keep the weave in place.

11.

Test out different textures when you paint by making your own paintbrushes! Hunt around for interesting objects that you'd like to paint with. Some ideas are....

Pompom

Feathers

Sponge

String

Fake grass

Leaves

Elastic
bands

Balloon

12.

Symmetrical leaves!

Create your leaves by painting onto coffee filters using inks or water-colour paints so create an abstract, merged effect. Let this dry, and then fold them in half. Now sketch a leaf template onto it. Remember, you only want to do half so that it's symmetrical. There are some templates here!

13. Experiment with colour and layers

Get some nice thick paints or even some crayons or oil pastels, and draw big blocks of colours.

Test out what colours you think look good together,

in this book I think yellow, pink, green and purple look good!

What colours are they? * This is fun, can you think up of a story for your final piece? Why did you choose those objects?

14. Mix together some salt dough clay with 1 cup of flour, 1 cup of table salt and half a cup of water. Mould it into any shape you like, and then and stick random found objects into it.

15. Make abstract plaster blocks!

For this, you'll need something plastic and disposable, so yoghurt pots are perfect for this idea!

With the help of an adult (because plaster gets very warm so shouldn't be touched , best handled by a grown up) mix together 1 part plaster to 2 parts water.

Make a few small amounts and add colour into them - you can do this by adding in blobs of acrylic paint, or pigment powders if you have them! Also try out other things, like food colouring, or even organic pigments like tumeric!

Then, grab your yoghurt pot and pour a little bit of one colour in. You can either wait for this to harden a bit or go straight in with another colour - experiment with how the layers merge and sit!

Don't touch the plaster as it sets - this is when it heats up and can be so warm it burns - so leave your masterpieces alone for 24 hours.

When it's fully hardened, carefully cut them out of the yoghurt pots.

How did they turn out?

What could you turn them into?

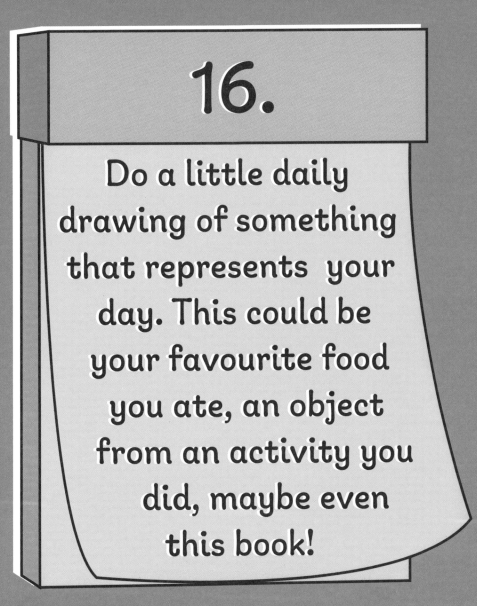

16.

Do a little daily drawing of something that represents your day. This could be your favourite food you ate, an object from an activity you did, maybe even this book!

17. Try out these recycled bottle sculptures! You can test out making a fish, a cactus or even a hybrid robot. What changes can you add to make it unique?

18. Have you ever tried tie-dye? Here's some cool folds and ways to gather a t-shirt or some fabric to get some super funky patterns. Give it a go!

19.
Paint blot pictures!
What can you see in these paint blots? Why don't you try making your own and then turning them into something!
Water down some acrylic paint so it's like cream and blob this into the middle of some paper. Then fold the paper in half and press down.
What sort of blob did you make?

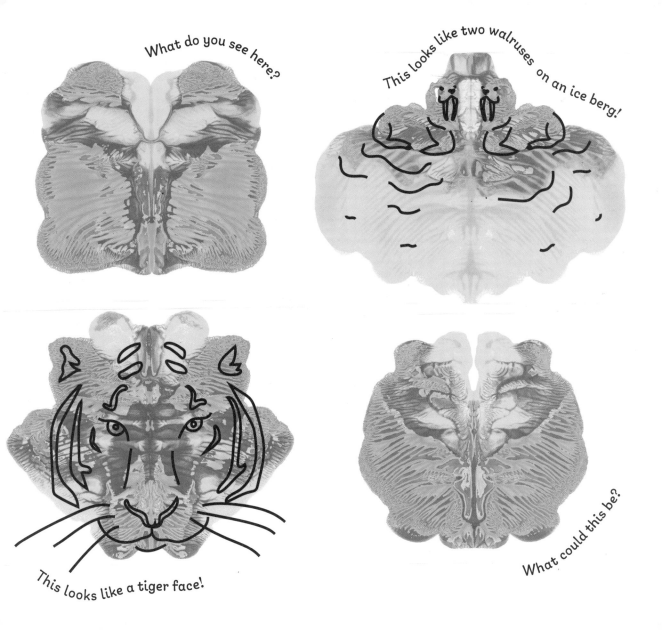

What do you see here?

This looks like two walruses on an ice berg!

This looks like a tiger face!

What could this be?

Take scraps and leftover bits of paper (the thinner the better - like newspaper or old magazines!) and tear or shred them into little pieces. Then, carefully cover them with boiling water in a bowl and let it soak over night. The next day, ask an adult to help you use a hand-blende and obliterate that mushy paper mixture! When it's all blended, squeeze out the water and put your pulp into a separate bowl. In the new bowl on squeezed pulp, add 1 part flour to 2 parts pulp. Mush this together with your

hands until it feels

mould-able clay.
make whatever
could form
around
create vases
just

like a firm,
Now you can
you like! You
the clay
moulds to
and cups, o
free-build!

20.
Make paper clay!

1.

2.

3.

4.

5.

(look at these bubbly reactions

21. Baking powder painting

Mix 2 tbsp of baking soda and add some liquid food colouring until you're happy with it's brightness. Then add another tablespoon or two to the mix, just so that it's not too runny. Paint it onto some thick paper - keep it abstract! Then, add a few drops of vinegar to different spots, and watch it fizz away!

Top tip!
So you know which section is which, start each new area using the opposite side of the bean to the one before.

What have you designed for your mosaic?

Mosaic art (with beans!)

Create an awesome artwork using beans and lentils in your cupboard! Draw an image (keep it quite simple!) and then fill in each section with the beans and lentils you find, sticking them down with PVA glue, best done on sturdy cardboard or even canvas! To add the finishing touch, paint over them with some poster paints or acrylics.

23. Marbling

To marble, you first need to get a tray or wide container and shallow fill it with cold water.

Then, take your marbling inks and drip little droplets onto the surface of the water. You'll see them expand and move about!

Add different colours and watch the pattern merge and change!

When you're happy, carefully place your paper onto the inks and slowly turn it over to reveal your design!

24. Weird and wonderful bioplastics

1tbsp cornflour
4tbsp distilled water
1tsp white vinegar
1 tsp glycerine
A few drops of food colouring

Mix everything together in a saucepan and heat steadily on a medium heat. Mix constantly, and you'll see it will start to thicken. Keep mixing until it goes clear and starts to bubble. This might take a little while! Once it looks like really weird jelly, spoon the mix onto some foil or parchment paper and smooth out with the back of a spoon. Put another piece of foil or paper over this and let it flatten underneath a pile of books or something else heavy and stable. If you want to, you could mix other things into the bioplastic, to add texture, or you could press flowers or leaves onto it after you've spooned it out.

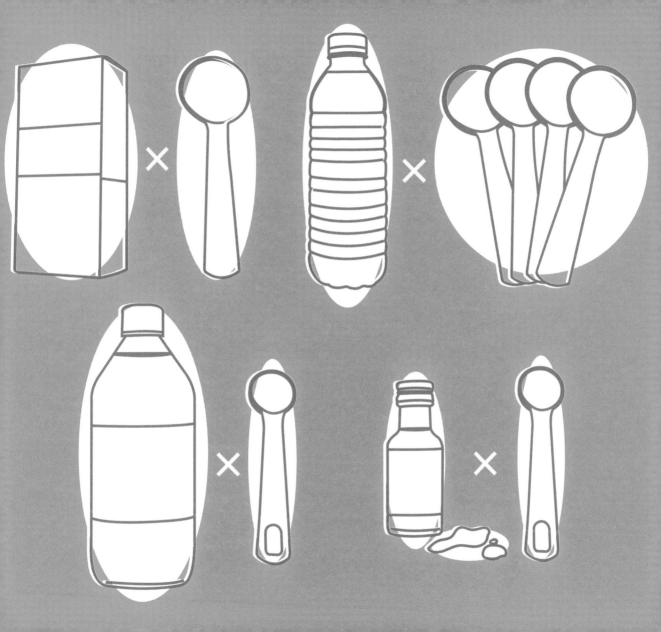

25. Natural Playdough

For this activity, make the dough the same way that you make the salt dough on page 30! To make all the different colours, try adding these cool natural ingredients. What could you use each different colour for?

Blueberries!

Coffee!

Red cabbage & baking soda!

Matcha powder!

Red cabbage & vinegar

Tumeric!

26.

Weaving with paper

When you weave with paper, you can play with different patterns and colours in a way that is much quicker & easier than with yarn! Try out some of these ideas and make sure to display your great artwork!

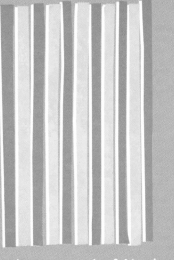

1. First, lay out your 'weft' in alternate colours, like green then yellow.

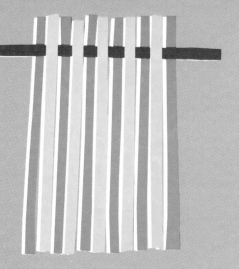

2. Then, start to weave with your first colour. Go over, under, over, under.

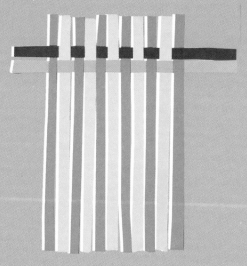

3. Then weave the next row with a new colour, and start under, over, under, over.

4. Continue this pattern to the end, doing the opposite to the row above!

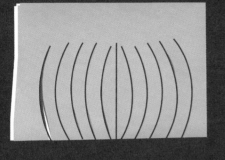

1. Start by folding your piece of paper in half and then cutting out the lines, shown here!

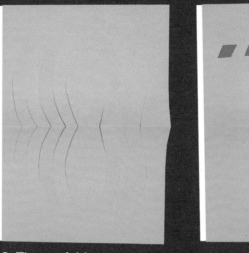

2. Then unfold your paper.

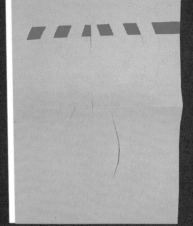

3. Now start weaving! Go under, over, under, to the end.

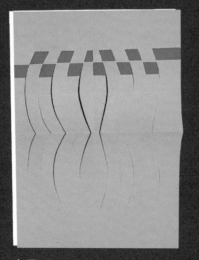

4. Then get a second strip and weave the next row, doing the opposite to the one above.

5. Repeat this all the way to the end and look! You have a 3D looking illusion!

What other kinds of patterns
and creations could you do?

What happens if you use strips
that are all different widths?

What kinds of shapes could
you cut your weaving into
if you stick it all together?

Or even weaving with images?

27. Leaf animals! Go out on a nice walk and have a look about for some funky shaped leaves! What different types of animal can you make with these shapes?

Can you ell what these animals are?

Top tip!
Try looking at the leaves + see what their shape reminds you of!

28. Flipbooks!

To make your own flipbook, you'll first need to start with lots of paper. You could use flashcards, a wedge of Post-it notes, or take some plain white paper and cut it into smaller pieces - probably best at around 10cm by 7cm. Gather all your paper together in one pile - you'll be grabbing from that lots as you go! - and do your first drawing.

It's usually easiest if this is some-thing that will stay still all through-out your animation, or will be easy to do the first movement from.

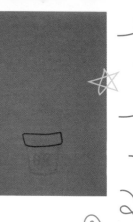

Now you've got your first drawing, you can get cracking with the next one!

Do this by putting your first drawing onto a light box, or even your computer screen or a window if it's bright outside. Place a new piece of paper over it, and trace the first drawing, but add the next bit - in my animation, this is the bud of a new leaf! What will yours be?

Carry on doing this for every newly drawn frame (that's what each piece of paper is called - it's an animation term!) until you have used up all your paper or you think your flipbook is complete.

Remember to keep progressing the animation as you go, and only exactly trace over things that are staying still.

You can then collect all your frames together, in order, and then tap them on a table on the short edge on the right, to make sure they're all in line for flipping through!

Now you have a whole flipbook! Try flicking through the pages – how does it look? Does it flow?

digital animation on your computer, using a video editing programme. Or, you could simply film your flipbook!

You could even scan in each frame and make a

(29) Drawing
what you feel

What feeling do you think this page is?

For this task, all you need to do is think about how you feel right now. Are you happy, excited, calm, maybe even *sleepy!*

How does this look if you were to draw it? Sometimes calm is light blue and happy is yellow polka dots and swirls!

30. Pop up origami & paper art!
Use these stencils to help you create some
cool pop-up origami! Cut on
the lines and then pull the middle of
the shape over to the X on the other side
of the page. Stick this down and you
should get some fun paper art! Try
it with
your
own
shapes!

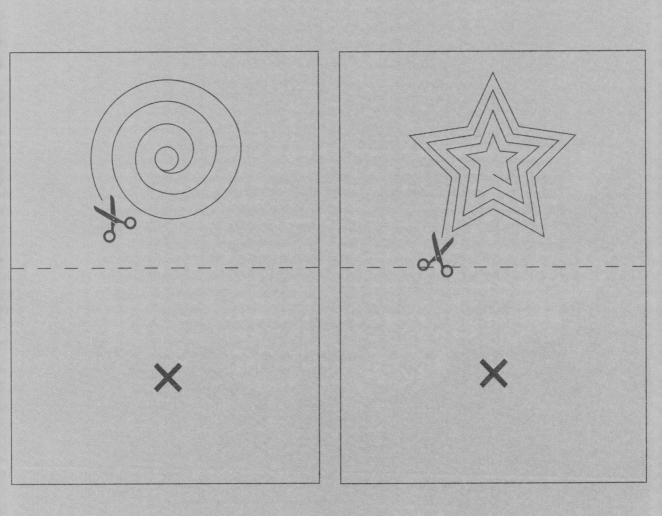

You can also try creating some fun abstract sculptures by building and combining these different paper sculpture techniques!

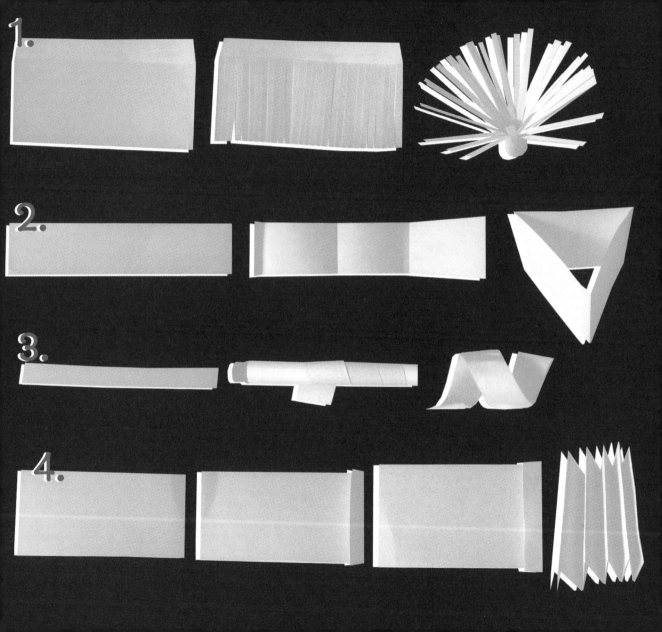

31. Experimenting with symmetry

Find images of bugs or leaves and recreate them by folding a piece of paper in half and cutting out one side of the shape.

Unfold the paper and see how your
symmetry is - does it look just
like what you copied? How well do
you know where the halfway point is?

32. Clay cane art

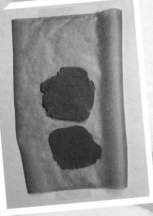

Start by flattening out your clay or plastercine. Use a rolling pin for this!

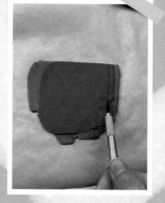

Then, layer them onto eachother. Carefull with a knife, cut the pieces

to the same size. It's OK if they don't completely line up!

Then, from one end, roll the clay up into a tube. Make sure to tuck it in!

Keep rolling until it looks like this. You could also try rolling it like a square!

Then, mark even pieces and, again carefully, use a knife to cut them out.

Usually you get a clean cut, and you'll be able to see a swirl in the tube!

Cut all the pieces and then lay them out flat in whatever way you like.

Get a piece of parchment paper and place your clay between it like this.

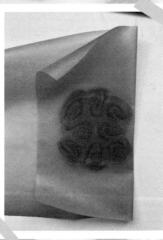

Firmly use a rolling pin to flatten out the pieces until they all merge!

Peel off your paper and look at the slab you made! What else can you try?

You will need:

Shoebox
A ruler
A craft knife
Black electric tape
Empty aluminium can
A sewing needle
Sandpaper
Black permanent marker
Darkroom photo paper

First, take your cardboard box and cut a small square, only a couple of centimetres squared, in the middle of the top flap or the lid of the box.

Do this by measure out the exact centre with your ruler and draw out the box first.

Use a craft knife to cut it out to keep it as accurate as possible.

You might want some help from an adult for this part!

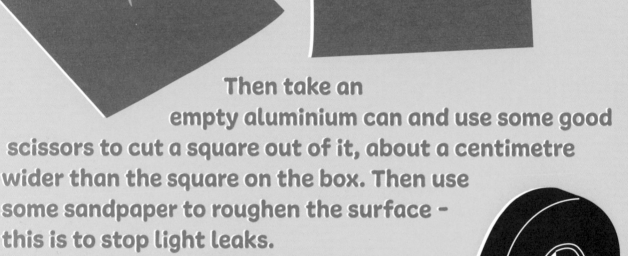

Then take an
empty aluminium can and use some good
scissors to cut a square out of it, about a centimetre
wider than the square on the box. Then use
some sandpaper to roughen the surface -
this is to stop light leaks.
Next, take a small needle an poke
a tiny hole in the middle. You
might need some help with this.

Next up, grab your electrical tape!

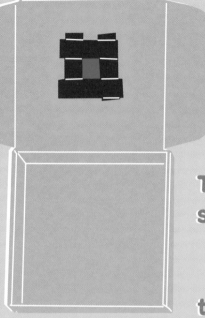

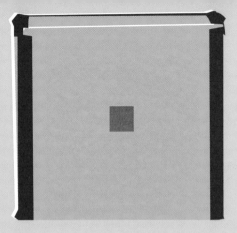

Tape the aluminium square over the square hole cut in the box lid.
Go to a dark or barely lit room & place your darkroom paper into the box. Now, using the black tape, tape around all the edges of the box to stop light leaks. You might want to put a tiny bit of tape right over the pinhole too.
Take your camera outside and lift the tape off the pinhole for a few minutes to expose it. Check it out!

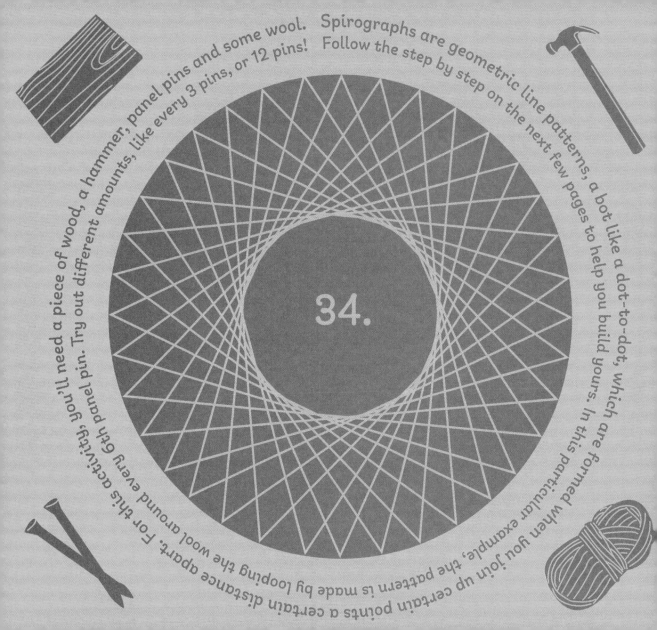

For this activity, you'll need a piece of wood, a hammer, panel pins and some wool. Spirographs are geometric line patterns, a bot like a dot-to-dot, which are formed when you join up certain points a certain distance apart. For this example, the pattern is made by looping the wool around every 6th panel pin. Try out different amounts, like every 3 pins, or 12 pins! Follow the step by step on the next few pages to help you build yours. In this particular example, the pattern is made by looping the wool around every 6th panel pin.

34.

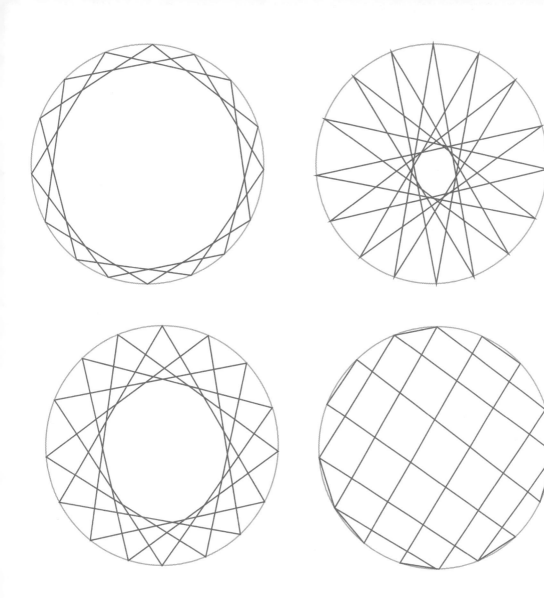

ice lolly pain

To make your own ice lolly painting, you need to squeeze some poster paint or acrylic paint into an ice cube tray and add a little bit of water to each cube. Mix each one with a lolly stick and let it sit upright in the paint mix. Put it in the freezer over-night and the next day, you have ice lolly paint! What will you paint?

35.

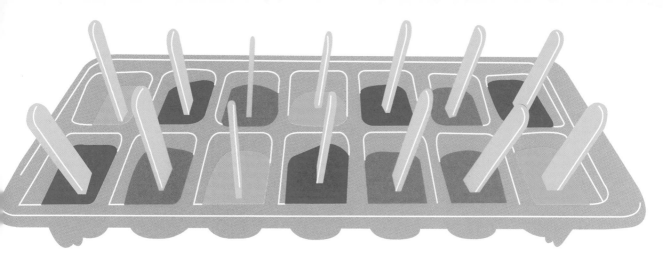

Very similarly, you could also just make cubes of ice paint without the sticks, and then place the ice paint onto some paper and let them melt and merge together into an abstract piece!

sun prints

To create a sun print, you need
to buy cyanotype paper and find objects
to make your print with. This could be leaves,
shells, even bits of paper or plastic! Place your
objects onto the paper and leave it out in the sun for
a minute or two, until the blue turns white. Then, you
need to rinse your paper under some water until it goes
blue again, and then let this dry! Look at the cool shadows!

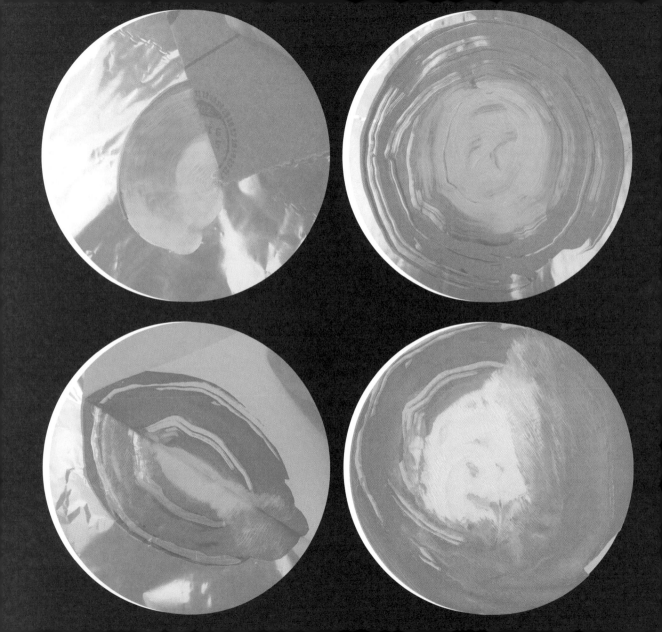

37.

Foil monoprints!

To create a foil mono-print, squeeze, splat, squish and smoosh some paint onto a piece of foil. You can do this in any shape, but circular is easiest to press out.

Then, place a piece of paper on top and press down - if you're feeling brave, you could roll over it with a rolling pin! Peel off your paper and check out the cool print you made! What kinds of patterns and colour merges did you achieve?

38. Screenprinting

An embroidery hoop

A pencil or marker

A piece of card

board

Fabric paint

A paintbrush

Some old tights

Sealing PVA glue

The first thing you'll want to do is stretch your tights over the embroidery hoop and tighten the screw at the top to hold it together tight. Trim off the excess tights fabric. Then, draw your design onto the tights that you want to print. Here I've done a tropical plant leaf!

Then, using a paintbrush, paint your sealant around your design. A thick PVA is good for this. The places that you paint with glue will not let the fabric paint through – so remember this when you put the glue onto the tights. Let this dry before the next step!

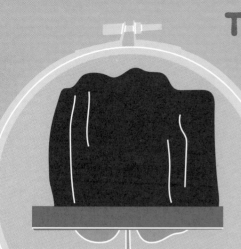

Take a blob of fabric paint and dollop it onto the tights. Then, using your piece of card board as a squeegee, scrape the paint over the screen and your design.

When you lift off your screen, you'll see your design left behind! You can now re-use this as many times as you like and print it onto things like bags, tops and canvases!

39. Zines

Zines are like mini magazines (a bit like how the word 'zine' is a mini version of maga'zine'!) & have been around for many years. They used to be called 'chapbooks', and would contain sections of novels, or even short stories. Now, they're cool DIY arty booklets!

This one is called an accordian because of how it folds. It springs in and out just like an accordian does!

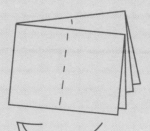
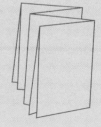

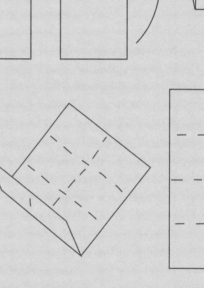

This is a bit tricker to make, but once you've done it, it's exactly like a mini book, with different pages that you can flick through!

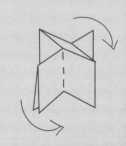

What will you put in your zine?

Maybe a comic?

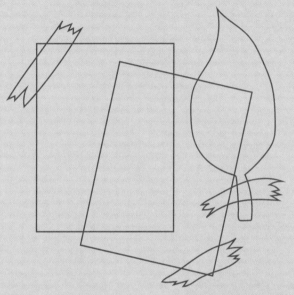

Or a scrapbook?

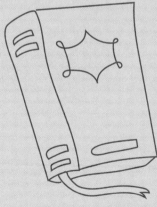

Or a story?

For these colour block
images, you'll need 2
pieces of
paper in

Colour Print

Images

different
colours.
You could try black
and white, or other
contrasting colours.

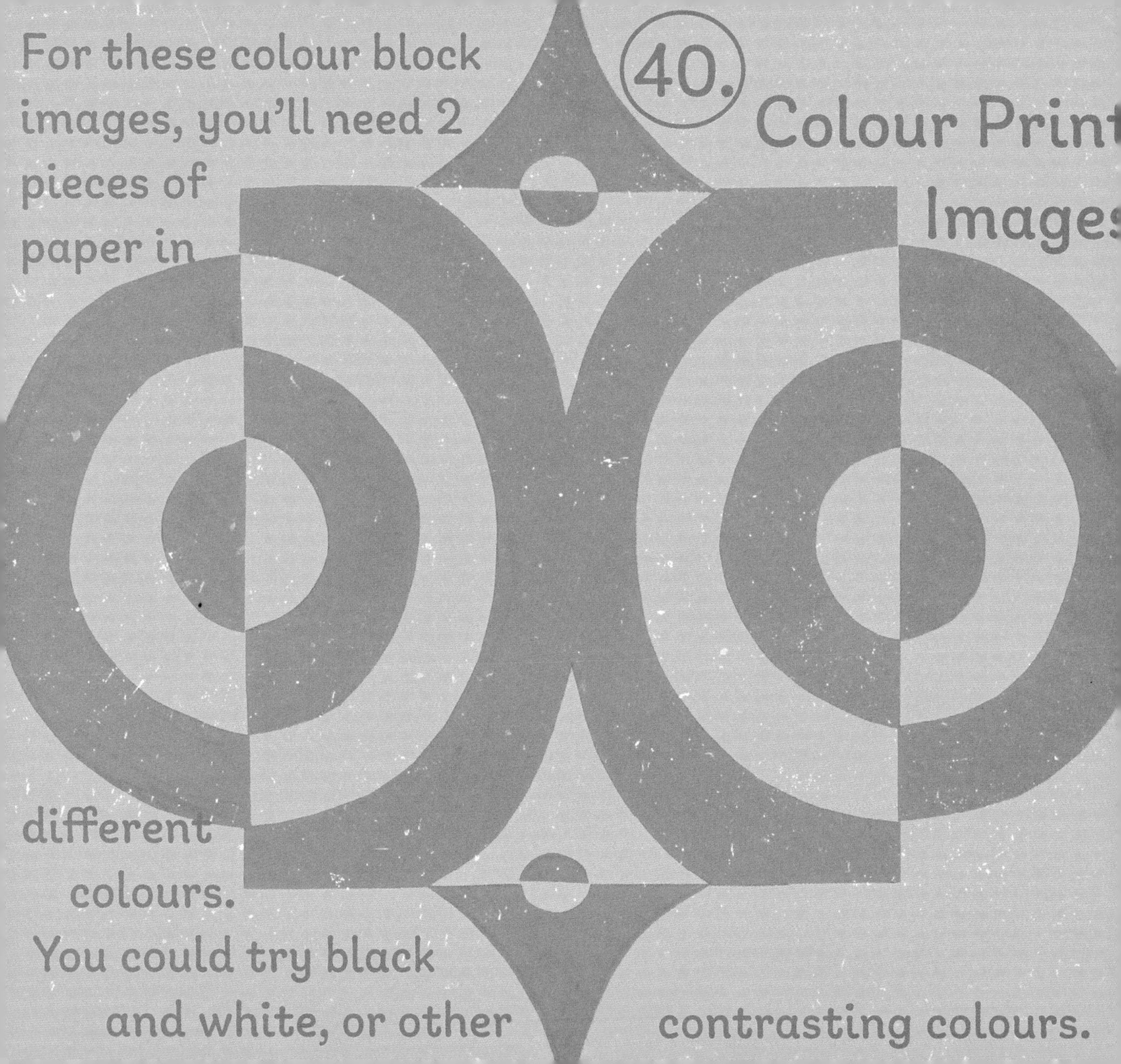

Draw your design on a square and then cut them out. You then need to flip it over so that it reflects on the other side.

Like this!

41. Foam sheet sculptures

Create abstract sculptures by starting with a small blob shape and slowly getting larger and larger with each layer of foam sheet - what could it look like? A melting candle, a stalagmite, a paint splodge?

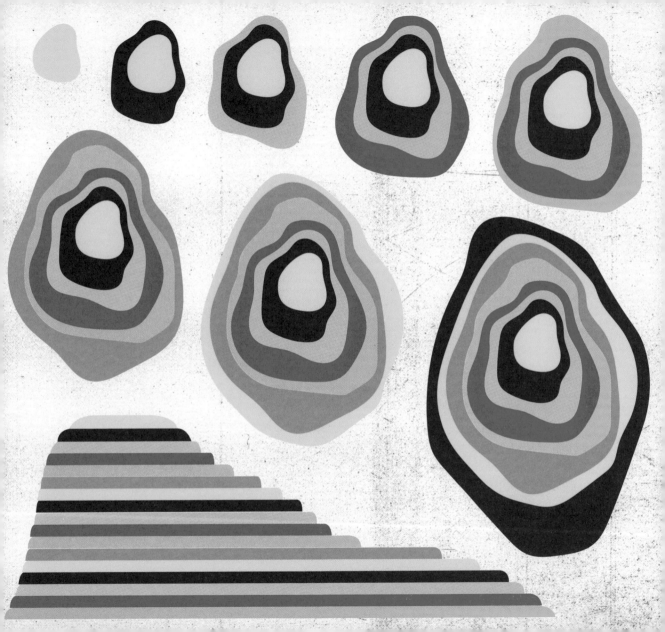

What you'll need:

Lay out your flowers or leaves onto your paper (petals face down) then cover with greaseproof paper

Now is the part where you grab your hammer and smash it onto the flowers!

When you've fully flattened them, peel off the greaseproof paper. Your flowers will look quite smooshed! Then, carefully peel them off too, and you'll get an effect like the one over this page!

43. Turning scribbles into things

Sometimes, the most fun way to start a drawing is to do a big silly scribble and then see what the shape reminds you of! What do these scribbles look like? What can you turn them into?

a pair of glasses maybe?

a blob fish?

a haircomb?

44. Clay slab building

Clay slab building is the technique of rolling out clay to an even thickness and then cutting shapes and joining together to create a 3D piece.

you'll need air dry clay, tools to cut & score the clay and some slip, which is made by mixing clay with enough water to cover it & leaving it to soak overnight.

How to - Mini Clay House

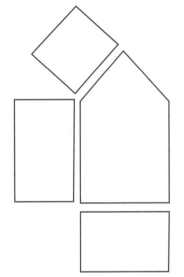

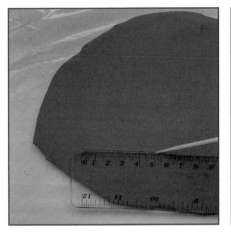

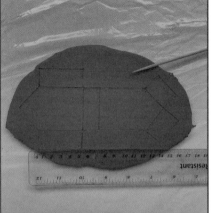

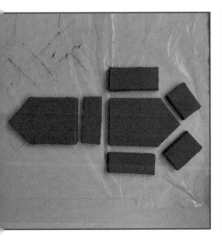

How to - Groovy Pot

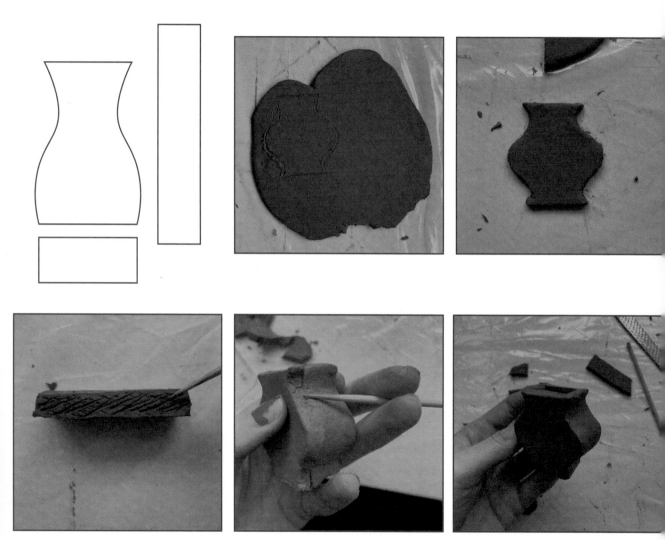

Pottery shapes

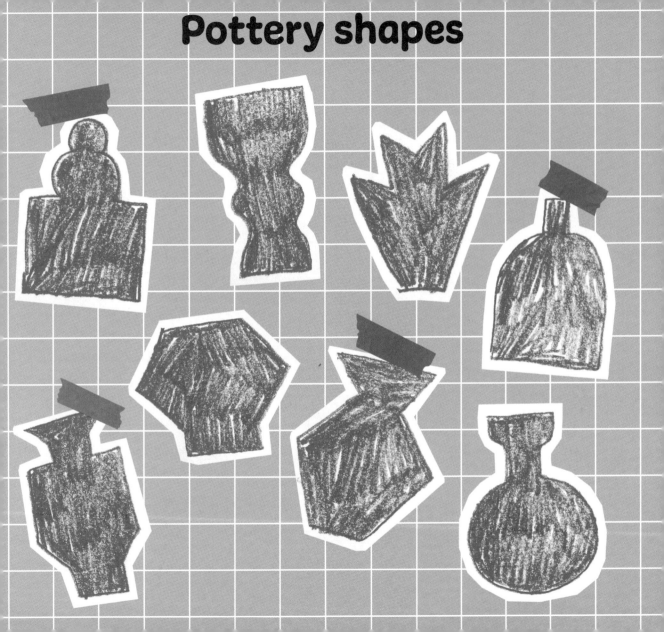

45. Bokeh

the word 'bokeh' comes from the Japanese word 'boke', meaning 'blur' or 'haze', & is the blurring of a photo (especially of lights) to create a beautiful effect. It's also super easy to do by yourself!

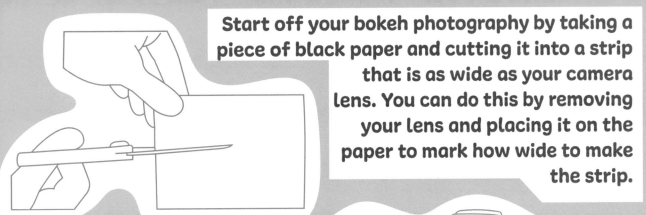

Start off your bokeh photography by taking a piece of black paper and cutting it into a strip that is as wide as your camera lens. You can do this by removing your lens and placing it on the paper to mark how wide to make the strip.

Then, wrap the paper around your lens and tape it into a circle.

Then, you need to figure out what size the end will be, which will go over the lens. Place your new lens cover onto a new piece of paper and draw around it.

Next, cut out the circle using some scissors. Take your pencil again and draw a rectangle onto the middle of the circle - this is where you will place your shape filters. cut this out with a craft knife (ask for help if you need to) and then use tape to stick the circle onto the lense cap you made earlier.

Now the fun part! Cut out some more squares, around the same size as the circle, and draw on the shape filters you want for your bokeh. You'll need to use a craft knife again to cut these out.

Ask for some help changing your aperture as wide as the camera will go (f/2.8) and to turn on the auto ISO sensitivity. Then, zoom out the lens as far as it will go and you are set to go!

First place your cap you just made over the lens. Make sure this fits on OK and doesn't disrupt the image - otherwise you might need help to fiddle a bit more with the camera settings.

Then, take your shape filters and hold them close over the lens cap and try taking photos! First the best results, try taking photos of fairy lights or car lights from a window.

I hope you feel super creative and proud of yourself.

you should show off your creations! I always love to see them.

Get someone to help you take a photo of what- ever you've made from this book and then ask them to post it using the tag

#creativeblockkids

Use these pages as a scrapbook to stick in your own creations!

I **made** this!

Awesome artwork!

stick here

stick here

Suuuuper proud of this!

Check **this** out!

stick here

stick here

WOW!

stick here

my amazing art

BIS Publishers
Borneostraat 80-A
1094 CP Amsterdam
The Netherlands
T +31 (0)20 515 02 30
bis@bispublishers.com
www.bispublishers.com
ISBN 978 90 6369 624 5